Ghosts of Rye
and things
that go bump in the night!

Thomas Peacocke Community College
Local History Group
Co-Ordinator and Editor:
Mrs Jo Kirkham

We have arranged the Rye Experiences in an order which can make a WALK

ISBN 1 870600 20 7

© **Jo Kirkham**
Thomas Peacocke Community College,
The Grove,
Rye, Sussex. November 1995.

Second Impression: January 2007

We are grateful to the following:
Sheila Draffin who allowed us to use her sketches on
pages 8, 17, 18, 20, 21
Brian Hargreaves for his drawing on page 5
Rye Town Council for that on the inside cover

INTRODUCTION AND ACKNOWLEDGEMENTS

A year ago, the members of the **Group** were divided into two sections, those working on **The History of Rye Hospital**, (published July 1995), and the rest investigating the **ghost stories** of the Rye area. **Andrew Tomkins** took charge of this part. Always in our investigations there is a point at which we have to say that extra information will be kept for the next edition, and this topic, more than others which we have presented, lends itself to 'My experience was . . . ', as soon as the subject is mentioned. We thank the members of the community and students in the College, for sharing their observations with us. Some are quite happy for their names to be used, but others felt reluctant, and we have respected their wishes. However, **every** story in the book, apart from the published ones from "A Chronicle of Rye" by L.Grant and those from "Winchelsea Memories" by K.Forbes-Duncan, were told to members of the Group. We also thank **Mrs Sarah Surman and Mr David Beale,** College Staff members, for their help, **Loraine Charman** for the cover design and **James Kirkham** for his technical expertise.

We offer no explanation for the stories, but noted that many ghosts come around All Souls Day, or Hallowe'en. Is there a spiritual connection? - souls who need rest? Are they just more noticeable in the dark winter nights? Many are associated with public houses. Why? Certainly the smugglers, so important in this area, played on susceptibilities of local people, to frighten them to keep them indoors, whilst they carried on their trade. The 'half' ghosts need investigation. Others, surely, are imagined.

CONTENTS

Introduction and Acknowledgements	3
Rye	6
Strand - Heritage Centre	6
Strand - Ship Inn	7
South Undercliff	7
Mermaid Street	8
West Street	12
Churchyard	13
Watchbell Street	14
Traders Passage	16
Church Square	17
Market Street	20
Lion Street	21
Conduit Hill	22
The Monk and his Lover Sightings	23
Turkey Cock Lane	23
Conduit Hill	26
Landgate	27
Hilders Cliff	27
High Street	27
Landgate	28
Fishmarket	28
New Road	28
Military Road	29
Deadman's Lane	29
Cinque Ports Street	30
Ferry Road	33
Needles Passage	34
High Street	34
Tilling Green	35
On Gibbet's Marsh	36
The Marshes Around Rye	36
Other Rye Ghost Stories	37

Stories from around Rye
Appledore	38
Ashford	38
Beckley	38
Biddenden	39
Brede	40
Broad Oak	44
Brookland	45
Camber	45
East Guldeford	46
Ewhurst	46
Guestling	48
Hastings	48
Icklesham	51
Iden	51
Lydd	52
New Romney	53
Northiam	53
Pett	54
Ruckinge	54
Rye Foreign	54
Stone-in Oxney	55
Udimore	55
Winchelsea	56
Wittersham	58

GHOSTS OF RYE AND THINGS THAT GO BUMP IN THE NIGHT!

★

RYE
THE STRAND - THE HERITAGE CENTRE

On the **Old Quayside** at **the Strand** in Rye, is the **Heritage Centre,** home of the Tourist Office and also the Rye Town Model and it deals with many people each year as an essential part of the Tourist Industry in Rye.

However it appears to house more of the history of Rye than the employees may have liked, for it appears to be the resting place for a ghost or even ghosts.

The visual aspects of the ghost were explained to us by **Mrs Joanna Arkley**, the Assistant Manager. She told us about the time she entered the building to open up for the day. In the half light she was confronted by a waist high, **black dog** with glowing, red eyes. Having run around to the opposite side of the counter and switched the lights on, she turned to look at whatever it was, but it had vanished!

In the **Old Sail Loft**, alongside the Exhibition of Rye's History, there is a representation of the butcher, John Breeds, who was hung in 1742 for killing the Mayor's brother-in-law. *[see page 14]* After hanging, he was put into an iron cage, and he swung on the Marsh for about 80 years. The only part of the original remaining is the skull, the rest having been secretly removed by arthritis sufferers in the town. (An infusion made by boiling water and a bone from a convicted felon was supposed to be of real benefit in alleviating the pain.) These remains are in the Town Hall.

However, the copy hanging in the **Heritage Centre,** consists of **the full skeleton** in a cage and it weighs about 50kg. It swings over a balcony about a foot away.

We thought it would be almost impossible to lift or turn around without the use of ladders and at least two, strong people to help. But as **Joanna** came out of the Office, the skeleton, which usually faces away from her, was not, it was 'looking' **at** her! The whole thing had been lifted off the hook and turned to face her. The next morning, when she returned, the cage was back as if it had never moved!!

The third incident was confirmed by **Mrs Mary Collen** and other staff. One day recently, at the end of a Model Show, a lady said she had seen the **figure of a man** leaning **over the Model** during the story of the monk.

THE SHIP INN, THE STRAND

Christine Locke told us "I was about five years old and it was around 8 o'clock one night. My mother and I were at the **Ship Inn**. No-one was upstairs at the time and we heard **footsteps** walking across the floor, above the ceiling. Someone went upstairs and the hairs on that person's neck and back, stood up on end. Now, whenever anyone goes upstairs, they go in pairs."

SOUTH UNDERCLIFF

Mrs T.Hodgson says "my house in **South Undercliff** has its ghost. It seems to be a happy, kind ghost and I feel quite safe. In December 1945 I moved there and, at a time when neither my husband nor I smoked, we sometimes smelled **tobacco smoke.** This was as we went past the back door and also as we went into the back bedroom. In fact I will swear I have **seen** smoke. A neighbour told me, after we had been living there about a year, that 'Old Captain Breeds' had shot himself in my house. When my husband was ill, I said I would have to sell, as I couldn't live in the house with a ghost by myself. My husband said 'Don't do that, he won't do you any harm!' and he hasn't! My son says he has seen an old sea captain in the house. The whole thing is very odd as I have a very poor sense of smell, and yet I <u>do</u> smell it!"

(See **RYE MEMORIES VOLUME 7** *:* ***Memories of My Town*** *- Ladies of the Women's Institute in 1953 and Eileen Bennett and Theresa Hodgson)*

MERMAID STREET

At **the foot of Mermaid Street**, a **man in a tall hat** has been seen crossing towards the antique shop, quite recently.

Mr Edwin Gibson told us of a visit to his friend **Mr Ament's** house, just above the shop at the bottom of **Mermaid Street**. The living room was upstairs and whilst he watched, a **picture** came off the wall and 'put itself' on the floor. No-one was near it at the time.

Mr Steve Denny lived on **the corner of Mermaid Street and Traders Passage,** in '**Oak Corner',** at one time and he said "There was a definite **presence** in that house. It had been part of a much larger house at one time which had been divided into three - and there were 'experiences' in all parts. I never saw anything, but I didn't like the feel of it. Many other people, including family members did see an old man in Jacobean costume. We were glad to get out of that house!"

Mrs Jenny Hadfield and her family, living at **Jeakes House** on **Mermaid Street**, had an elderly gentleman living with them for some years. A few weeks after his death, the window cleaner, on knocking at the door to be paid for his work, remarked that he had washed all windows, with the exception of the window of the room where the **old gentleman** was asleep!! No one had occupied that room since his death!! A guest in the house has also seen **'Uncle Malcolm'**.

Between this house and the one on **the opposite side of the street**, **two ladies in long dresses** have been seen crossing the street, very regularly, and by many people.

Another friend is able to see across the Street, into the house opposite. She has seen, on several occasions, a **woman wearing blue,** and with an old fashioned wimple head dress! This was confirmed by yet another person whose bedroom it was, and who described the woman as, a "presence", a "healing, herb woman", who seemed "good".

Another informant told us of the top **half of a woman** being seen at a window, with a space below her. This seemed strange. but then architectural investigation of the property showed that the windows had been enlarged in the last century. The 'half' missing from the spectre would have been below the old window sill.

Many people saw these ghosts and eventually some of the houses were blessed, and in those buildings they have not been seen since.

The Mermaid Inn is very ancient and was re-built, after the French burned and sacked the town in 1377, on top of the Medieval cellars. It has several ghosts and reports of strange happenings associated with it. Some of these incidents are taken from a paper produced by **Mrs Judith Blincow** and we thank her for her permission to use information from it.

Many famous personages have stayed at the **Inn,** including Lord Alfred Douglas (Oscar Wilde's 'Bosey'); F.E. Smith, the great advocate; Henry Dodge, the American motor car magnate and Ford Maddox Ford, the novelist. Visitors have included Dame Ellen Terry, the actress, and also the writers Hilaire Belloc, Henry James, Rupert Brooke, Ben Travers and E.F. Benson as well as members of the Royal Family.

During the 1930's a fascinating ghost story came to light. There had been rumours of a haunting in the **Elizabethan Chamber** (now

Room 16) on October 29th and one year, a lady claiming to be a psychic, asked to sleep in the room that night. **Miss Aldington** joined her. The lady slept well, but during the night, **Miss Aldington** awoke to find **a silent duel** raging around her. The combatants were dressed in doublets and hose, and fighting with rapiers. They fought for several seconds until one received a fatal sword thrust. The victor looked nervously around the room, dragged the bleeding body of the other combatant to a trap door in the corner of the room and he disposed of the body by throwing it down into a secret passage. This passage would have let the body land in the **Bar** section.

A few years ago, **the Barman** was tending to his fire, when all the **bottles** on the bottle shelf at the other end of the room fell off. He handed in his notice the next day!

There were more **secret ways**, apart from the present staircase between the Bar and Dr Syn's room. Found to date are a moving panel in Room 18 and an entrance to the 'Priest's Hole', through the back of the cupboard above the Bar fireplace.

The **Hawkhurst Room** (Room 18) is a double one with a single adjoining. An American lady, sleeping in the single room, reported that a **gentleman in old-fashioned clothes**, sat on her bed during the night. When he would not go away, she pulled her mattress into the double room where her sons were sleeping and stayed there until morning.

In **The Nutcracker Suite** (Room 5), a **Lady in white** walks through from the single room across the main room and through the door, stopping at the foot of the bed for a moment on her way past.

Room 1 is called **Cadmans** and there are lots of reports of a **lady in white or grey** who sits in the chair by the fireplace. Guests, many weeks apart, have told the same story of leaving their clothes on this chair during the night and, when they have awoken in the morning, they have found their **clothes all wet**. There are no windows or pipe-work anywhere near the chair.

The **Lady in white** is supposed to be a girl working in the Mermaid in the 1700's who fell in love with a smuggler. She was then murdered by them for talking too much about their exploits. She wanders the corridors of the Inn looking for **her** smuggler.

In **Fleur-de-lys,** (Room 10), two years ago, a bank manager and his wife were woken up to find **a man** walking through their bathroom wall and across the centre of their room. They were so frightened that they spent the rest of the night downstairs in the lounge and made the porter bring all their luggage downstairs, plus their clothes.

The Kingsmill, (Room 17), has had many incidents in it. It seemed to go **terribly cold** and a **rocking chair** in the room would rock for no reason. The chambermaids would only clean the room in pairs as they didn't like to be there by themselves.

Miss Kathleen Sherwood, told us of the following experiences she has had whilst working at **The Mermaid.**

"A young girl started changing the bed and then ran to me in the linen room. '**A rocking chair** is moving on its own - quite fast too - and I didn't touch it!' I said she must have done so, but then I went into the room with her. The chair was still, but as I watched it, it began to rock and the **cushion** on it squeezed down as if a fairly large person was sitting on it!"

People, who stayed in the room a couple of nights afterwards, heard footsteps walking round the bed, but there was no-one there.

The room next door had strange happenings too! Visitors went to sleep with the **TV on a table,** yet, when they woke up, it was on the floor! People also heard strange **scratching noises** on the wall next door.

These incidents all happened at the end of October and we wondered if there was a connection with Hallowe'en - All Souls Day."

Miss Georgie Pinwill told us : "When I was living at the **Inn**, I was lying in bed, when all of a sudden, '**someone'** sat on the side of it next to me - but no-one was there!"

Miss Kate Davis was working as a chambermaid there and one morning she was walking along a corridor. **A lady** was coming in the opposite direction and, as they passed each other, Kate said "Good-Morning!" There was no reply, and so Kate turned round to look at her, but there was no-one there and no door for her to have gone through!

Annabelle Alstin and Jessie Franklin say the **Mermaid** has a ghost upstairs, who **walks across the landing** from Room No.1 to Room No.3.

Alena Spencer said "I was in an old house on **Mermaid Street**. We were on a Ghost Expedition. We were going down into **the cellars** and there was not much light - it was kind of creepy! My friend and I decided to go another way to the others. I looked over my shoulder because I thought someone was following us. The cellar was supposed to be haunted by the crew of a small smuggling ship who had been killed down there. We got to a dead end and we decided to go back. Just then it became really **cold and icy** and we just ran. We stopped with laughing because we thought how stupid we had been. Then I thought someone was watching me and I saw **a shadow** on the wall. We ran back to the group. We were told we had been in the chamber of the captain, who had been killed last - it seems he always walks up and down the corridor looking for spies!"

WEST STREET

Mr M.Fannon used to live in **West Street** as a boy, opposite the "Old Custom House". He recalls people being afraid as they heard **chains being dragged along** a hard floor as they passed by.

Lamb House has several ghosts. Very recently a lady tourist, in quite a matter of fact way, described an **old lady in Victorian dress** who was sat in a chair in the corner whilst the visitors went round.

Many people have seen her. The Editor remembers **Mrs Tomlin,** who worked as cook for E.F.Benson, describing her at a Women's Institute meeting.

Canon Fowler, Vicar of Rye and father of Mrs Warrender, together with **E.F.Benson**, both saw a ghost one summer afternoon whilst sitting in the **Secret Garden of Lamb House**. It was a man **dressed in black clothing** with hose and throwing his cloak over his shoulder with a flick. They both said they saw the apparition at other times.

Miss Stella Pigrome's father used to play chess with **E.F.Benson** and tells of the first time he visited the **Garden Room** of Lamb House.

"Do you mind sitting in that chair?" said Mr Benson. "No, I am quite comfortable, thank you." Mr Pigrome replied. "That was the chair **Grebell** died in - I often **see him in it**." came the answer.

    Mrs T.Hodgson told us that, on one occasion, some Americans spoke to **Mr Fred Parris** and asked to take his picture outside **Lamb House**, where E.F.Benson was living. They took his address and forwarded him a print. In the photo which they sent to him was the picture of a **little old lady** in one of the windows - <u>no-one</u> had been in the house at the time! Mr Benson confirmed that story!

    Mrs Rhodes tells of **"Farleys Ghost"**, **near Lamb House.** In the 1930's **Mr Parris** saw **two ladies** going into **Lamb Cottage**, both being "see through" and one wearing a mantilla. He was concerned about it and knocked to ask if anyone of that description was staying there. The answer was "No"! He returned and saw them again and managed to take a photograph of them This was reproduced in the "Daily Standard" in the late 1930's.

THE CHURCHYARD

    A memorial in the Clare Chapel, in St. Mary's Parish Church, records the fate of Allen Grebell, the Deputy Mayor: "who fell by the cruel stab of a sanguinary butcher, March 17th, 1742".

    The butcher, John Breeds had mistaken Allen Grebell for his brother-in-law, James Lamb, who was the Mayor. Having been fined for selling meat at short measure by James Lamb in his capacity as chief Magistrate, John Breeds swore to get his own back on him.

    He lay in wait in the Churchyard one dark night, for the Mayor, who had been dining on his sons' ship tied up at the Quay, to return to his home, Lamb House. On hearing footsteps coming across the Churchyard, Breeds jumped out from behind a tomb stone and stabbed the passer-by.

    Unfortunately for him, the Mayor had felt unwell, possibly with one of the frequent attacks of marsh fever, (a kind of malaria), which was prevalent in this area at that time, before many of the Marshes were drained. He had asked his Deputy to stand in for him at the dinner, so the unfortunate victim was Allen Grebell, and not James

Lamb. He did not die immediately, but staggered to his home, opposite to Lamb House, and bled to death before being found next morning.

The culprit was easily found, for, not only had Breeds been swearing vengeance on the Mayor, but he had gone around shouting "Butchers should kill lambs! Butchers should kill lambs!", at the top of his voice.

His knife, covered in blood, was found behind the tombstone, where he had laid in wait. He was held in the Prison in the Castle or Ypres Tower, until his trial for murder. Although James Lamb had been advised not to try the case, by London lawyers, he decided to do so, and thus made history, by trying the man who had tried to murder him!

Both **John Breeds** and **Allen Grebell's** ghosts have been seen in the **Churchyard**. Reproduced on the inside front cover is the drawing of the ghost of **John Breeds**, "as sketched from memory, by G.Goddard on 20 April 1882". The original sketch is in the Town Hall.

Mr Richard Horner says that the **Grebell ghost** haunts the **Lamb family** - and it was this that made him study the maritime history of the period, and come to a different explanation for the reasons behind the murder. [See Rye Memories Volume 20 : RYE SHIPPING].

Mr W. Cutting told us that a "**Headless Sailor**" has been seen in the **Churchyard**, but he thought a lot of the ghost stories were put out by smugglers, who wanted to frighten people and get them to stay in at night,.

Miss Pat Aldington's sister told **Mrs Rachael Sarrediene** of an occasion when she was walking across the **Churchyard** on the diagonal path from Watchbell Street to the Church. She followed **a lady** who she thought was inappropriately dressed for the cold winter dusk - in a grey dress and no coat. The lady just walked on and disappeared into the chimney of the house next to the pink Old Vicarage.

WATCHBELL STREET

Mrs Geraldine Bromley told us that she had felt a definite presence in the **first house in Watchbell Street**, **next to Church Square**, when she lived there about 1980.

Mrs Monica Oliver used to live in **Watchbell Street** and she told us that her house had a ghost which they saw for the four years that they were there. **A little boy** dressed in a white kimono type gown used to come in and lean on her bed. It resembled a picture on her son's bedroom wall and he saw it too, on many occasions, and he used to come in to her bedroom to tell her that he'd seen the boy **again**.

The owner of **another house** in **Watchbell Street** related to us a story of the 1930's, which was confirmed by **the Misses Alma and Sylvia Fabes**. The cook had her afternoon off and she walked along to the **Look-Out Terrace** at the end of the Street. As she was sat on the seat, she had the feeling she was not alone. **A monk** in a brown habit appeared beside her and she was so frightened that she ran off - back to her kitchen. When she got there she found the monk had got there before her. The monk, when reproached by the cook for invading her kitchen, replied "But I live here. At least, I am buried in your garden."

He was articulate and he told her what was troubling him. He had been brought from Canterbury to discipline some dissolute monks in Rye. However he had been murdered, by being hit on the back of the head, for his efforts, and his body had been secretly buried in the garden of the house in Watchbell Street. He desperately wanted to be buried in consecrated ground.

The cook told her mistress, a devout Roman Catholic, about the ghostly monk, and she related the tale to Father Bonaventure, the Franciscan Monk in charge of St. Anthony of Padua Roman Catholic Church at that time. He decided that to try to find bones would be a very difficult task and so he blessed the whole garden. This monk has not been seen again.

Several people told us that a **'Sailor'** haunts the **Hope Anchor Hotel; Misses Alma and Sylvia Fabes** recounted the story told by **Miss C.Bellhouse**, who opened the **Hope Anchor Hotel** in 1935. "Night after night in late summer, around 4 am, she and her receptionist would hear the patter of **footsteps** approaching the hotel from Watchbell Street. Greatly mystified, they decided to stay up one night and keep watch, but although they did so for several nights, their vigilance remained unrewarded. The footsteps still hurried past the hotel, but only the shadows of scurrying clouds were visible in the moonlight."

'**Monks'** haunted the **house next door to the Hope Anchor**. **Miss Ella Harvey** said the owner told her that monks came to his door, wringing their hands in distress, and pointing to the cliff. It was believed that the house had once been a lodging place for monks of the Carmelite Friary. Just after he told her this, the "Green Steps" which lead down to the Strand Quay were being repaired, and during the works, human bones were dug up. They were passed on to the Vicar who buried them in the Churchyard and the monks were seen no more. *[See RYE MEMORIES : Volume 9].*

TRADERS PASSAGE

Miss Bellhouse, who owned the Hope Anchor Hotel in the 1930's, said several people, including herself, had heard **footsteps,** going down **Traders Passage,** but no one was ever visible.

Miss Alma Fabes told us of the ghost of an Elizabethan girl, who wandered up and down **Traders Passage**. Many saw her. The tradition was that on the Queen's visit to **Rye** in 1573, her **hand maiden** lost the Queen's black pearls there and she was seen, for centuries, looking for them.

This tradition was confirmed as a true 'folk memory' as **Miss Sylvia Fabes**, recounted that, in 1940, during the last War, a bomb was dropped on **Traders Passage** and part of the supporting wall fell down the cliff onto Strand House, situated immediately below. A workman clearing up the rubble found "what he considered to be a string of black beads of no value and took them to give to his little daughter. Delightedly she wore them, pleased with her father's find. A few days later a stranger stopped the little girl and enquired as to who had given her the beads. The child took the stranger home to see her father, who told the man how he had found them whilst clearing away the rubble. The stranger then told the story that these seemingly cheap baubles were in fact a string of priceless black pearls and from the shape of the clasp they were recognised as a family heirloom belonging to one of the oldest families in England." He was a London jeweller and he confirmed their authenticity.

Did the pearls belong to the Queen or to one of her ladies in Waiting? The pearls were sold and the ghost of the hand maiden looking for them walks no more!

CHURCH SQUARE

On the **corner of Watchbell Street and Church Square** there used to be **a pawn shop**. **Scratching noises** used to be heard on Friday evenings when the staff worked late, and these got louder week by week. The manager and his assistant decided to stay behind one Friday night to try to identify the noise. They became aware of a glow, together with the noises behind the barred window at the back of the shop. They got a shock when the light firmed up to be a **monk with a yellow face** staring in through the bars. The manager rushed at it with a stick and it disappeared. It would appear again for several weeks at a time and then vanish for a few months before re-appearing.

Misses Alma and Sylvia Fabes confirmed this tale, adding that when "this story was told at a meeting of the Rye Literary Society, it was found that one of the lady members had purchased the house some years before. She recounted how, when alterations she had planned were carried out, bones were discovered under the staircase." These were buried in the Churchyard and the monk has not been seen since. *[This property is between two parts of the Friars of the Sack remaining! Ed.]*

Miss Ella Harvey told us, that **Mr Leopold Vidler** related to her how, at **his house in Church Square, Friars of the Sack, a door** on an upper floor was always open in the mornings, "no matter how it was locked, bolted or screwed up at night!!"

The Misses Fabes said "Several of the houses in **Church Square** are reputed to be haunted by quite pleasant ghosts, one being the **ghost of a music master** who can be seen carrying his violin case down the narrow passages. Another is of a **very charming lady** who appears in the **Churchyard** late at night, and on being questioned as to why she is in the **Churchyard** at such a late hour replies, 'I love this little place, Rye, and I come back every now and again to see it.'"

Mr Edwin Gibson says that his wife felt '**something**' stroke her arm twice one night when he was away. His son saw a **girl in old fashioned clothes** in his bedroom - both incidents were in **St. Anthony.**

The house adjoining his, (on Watchbell Street), also had a ghost and several residents told of seeing it.

Daniel Britton's Aunt told him "Many years ago, I lived in a very old house in **Church Square.** I wasn't really happy living there, as it was very creepy. One day I was doing the house-work in the lounge, which had a very large fire-place. I was over the other side of the room, when, all of a sudden, as I turned around, I saw this figure of **a nun** sauntering slowly across the room. I just stood there transfixed. I couldn't move for a while, not believing what I had just seen. I thought perhaps it was a dream, but it wasn't. I told my family what I had seen and they didn't believe me. They just laughed."

A friend of the Editor, who lives in **Church Square**, told her that when her daughter was small, the child slept in the front room of the house and had frequent nightmares. One night, after waking screaming, the little girl was taken into her Mother's bed and still cried, pointing to her Mother's **feet.** The next day she enquired and found that a crippled child had lived in the house and she had had deformed feet! They had the house blessed, changed the child's bedroom and the nightmare's ceased.

Mrs Dorothy Wood said that her bathroom, in her house in **Hucksteps Row,** was always **icy cold**, despite any heating.

Mrs Pat Meyer told us that her neighbour on **Hucksteps Row** has said to her "Can you **smell fish**?". The answer was "No!" but, this used to be the fishermen's quarter!

Miss Harvey recounted that, late one night, as she turned the **corner of Church Square and Pump Street**, she thought she saw **something white** rising above the **Churchyard wall**. She took to her heels and ran all the way down Lion Street, until she reached her front door in the High Street, (now Penny Royal).

A corner of Church Square, Rye

'**The lady of the Methodist Church**', on the corner of **Church Square**, has been seen by **Mrs Sheila Miller**. One Wednesday evening, having opened up the Lower Hall for the **Ryesingers** practice rehearsal, **Mrs Anne Whiteman** heard someone go through the outside door. She went to see who it was, but there was no one there. **Mrs Miller** was coming **to** the Church for the choir practice, and saw a lady "in ordinary clothes" coming up the steps. Another choir member, **Mrs Elspeth Wrenn,** walking by Mrs Miller, saw nobody! Many times, when in the Lower Hall, choir members have thought someone was going in or out, but nobody is ever there.

MARKET STREET

Mr and Mrs Alan Webb, although sceptical about ghosts, said they could not explain an odd happening at their shop, **the Old Tuck Shoppe.** The shop is always cleaned and tidied at the end of the day, but several times, they found a sweet from the **centre** of the children's sweet table in the middle of the floor as they came in early in the morning. No-one had been in the building in the night and it had not been knocked off the edge of the table.

Mrs Tracy Masters, who had a Saturday job at that shop, said that some of other girls who worked there were reluctant to go upstairs. They told of **'a lady in grey'** who walked down from the attic floor to the first floor, where they used to get changed. She never saw anything.

LION STREET

Mrs Joyce Booth saw 'a figure', float past **the North Door** of **Rye Parish Church** as she waited outside after the rehearsal for the Memorial Service for **Dr. Alec Vidler.** The monk, head bowed, was dressed in a russet full-length gown and hood and he just disappeared.

Fletcher's House is a lovely old property, built about 1430. It was a private house for centuries and is believed to have been the birthplace, in 1579, of playwright John Fletcher, son of Richard Fletcher, Vicar of Rye, who was a contemporary of William Shakespeare. The building, now a coffee shop, is a three floored construction with the main restaurant on the bottom floor and private rooms above.

There have been at least two ghost sightings in the building. In 1951, **Mrs Betty Howard**, sister of the then owner, was working at the top of the building. She heard **footsteps** coming up the second flight of stairs. Thinking it was a customer, she opened the door and saw **a young man** standing on the landing a few feet below her. He was at least six feet tall, dressed in a dark coloured Edwardian suit, and about thirty years of age. She spoke to the stranger and the 'being' just faded away. She didn't feel him to be a frightening personage.

Several times since **footsteps** have been heard walking up the stairs. **Sam Jones**, who lives there now, told us. "Since I started working in the shop, many of the customers had asked me if I had seen a ghost, as they had seen reports that there was one. I had always dismissed these rumours until I saw what I believe to be '**The Fletcher's Ghost**'. I had just finished working my shift downstairs and I climbed the stairs to go back to my room. I arrived at the top and looked up to the third floor and saw what I thought must have been **a shadow**. Thinking it was my sister, I climbed the second flight of stairs to talk to her. When I arrived there, I saw an **old man dressed in a top hat and tails,** which looked to be Victorian. I immediately assumed that the man had got lost when looking for the toilets, but, by the time I had time to think, the man had travelled into our private bathroom. I followed him into the room, but when I went in, the man had disappeared, and all I could see, were what appeared to be tiny dots in the primary colours, hovering around the room, which then slowly dispersed as I entered. I have looked this phenomenon up and, according to various sources, the dots are supposed to be the sign of a good spirit rather than a poltergeist. This was early in 1995.

CONDUIT HILL

Mr Fred Parris used to live in the **cottage next to the Monastery**. This is reputed to be so haunted that, since his death, no one else will live there. He used to tell how he would be sitting there and **a ghost** would come and go through the door.

Another time, he went up to the Union Inn for a drink. Some friends called for him after he had left, and, though there had been no answer, all the **lights were on** and blazing out into the dark. Fred said he had definitely turned out all the lights before leaving.

Mr Parris was the caretaker of **the Monastery** when it was the Church Hall. He used to say there was a **poltergeist** in the building. Many times, when he was on his own in there, an icy wind would blow around him, but he could never see anything which could have caused it.

THE MONK AND HIS LOVER GHOSTS

TURKEY COCK LANE

This **narrow lane joining Hilders Cliff with Conduit Hill** has long been haunted. It is actually the top of the Town Wall and one can still look over into the Town Ditch, now the gardens of the houses on Tower Street, and they are at a much lower level.

The events and story which gives rise to the ghosts are associated with a fourteenth century Friar, **Brother Cantator**, (whose function was to lead the singing in the services in the Monastery), who fell in love with **Amanda.** She lived in a house situated where Tower House (or the Dormy House) now stands. The lovers used to meet secretly, for their love was not allowed, but eventually they were discovered. There seem to be several versions of the punishment imposed. One is that they were condemned to death and were walled up together - alive!

L.A.Vidler (in *A New History of Rye)* says they were buried alive. "Of course, they could not, after such treatment, rest quietly in their grave and Amanda was frequently seen flittering, white faced and white robed, in the windows of her father's house, now reputed to be haunted, while Cantator strutted up and down the lane in the form of a turkey cock, gobbling his old love songs to her. However, in the year 1850, the South Eastern Railway, while digging foundations, came across their skeletons, still clasped in each other's arms, and again the authorities were approached and this time it was decided to give them Christian burial, and never since have they been seen or heard by mortal eyes or ears."

Another explanation is that of the more usual punishment for this 'crime', that Cantator was 'immured', in other words he would live out the rest of his days in a minute cell, forbidden to communicate with the outside world in any way and be fed only through a tiny hole in the door. His mental state collapsed under these conditions and for a few days before his death, he became delirious and gobbled like a turkey. (In those days 'turkeys' as we know them, had not been brought to England and 'turkey' meant the noisy pea-hen). These **weird spine chilling sounds** have been heard by a number of people over the years.

Mr Vidler was certainly incorrect in saying that they (Amanda and Cantator) were now at rest. The Group have come across several people who have experienced the sight and sounds of them.

Mrs Rosalind Webb, whose home was on **Turkey Cock Lane**, now **Devonport House**, told the Editor that she had had experiences of Cantator there. Her whole family and visitors, regularly heard **footsteps** going up and down stairs.

One day **Mrs Webb** pushed **a door** and it wouldn't open. She thought it was her sons, but it wasn't. She tried again and suddenly it gave way, and **a shadow** moved by her.

The house had a door downstairs leading from the kitchen to **the pantry**. It used to swing open and stay open because it was on a slant. One day she came from the shop and aimed to open the door with her foot, but it swung back shut. She tried three times, before it opened as usual, and again, she felt **something brush past her**. She regarded it as a friendly ghost.

Mrs Pat Ciccone was asked to stay at the house, before she was married. She said "**Alan (Webb)** and **John (Ciccone)** were upstairs and **Mrs Webb** was across the landing. My room, on the corner of Conduit Hill and Turkey Cock Lane, had a cupboard on one side of the bed and a door the other side, beside a table with a 'teasmade' on it. **Something in the cupboard** woke me in the night. I leaned over to put on the light, but activated the 'teasmade' and woke the whole house up. The next morning I apologised for disturbing everyone. I said someone had woken me - **a 'presence'.** 'Oh, that's Charlie', they said. It seems that they all knew of it and 'Charlie', as they called 'Cantator,' used to come whenever there was someone new in the house, looking for his love. I never slept in that house again. I had never heard the story of the Monk and so was not anticipating anything happening.

My daughter **Joanna** had the same experience when she stayed in that house for the first time too." **Mr John Ciccone** confirmed the story and said he had heard the **footsteps** many times - and it wasn't just **Mr Len Webb** going out to work early as a baker!

Early in 1971, **Graham Rhodes,** one of the two milkmen delivering to **Turkey Cock Lane**, was astounded to see the **brown robed figure of a monk** at the end of the road adjoining the Landgate. He shouted to **Arthur Pope,** his colleague, who glanced up and 'nearly froze'. Watched by the two men, the ghost continued for a second or two until disappearing near the **Old Forge** opposite.

Mrs Sue Manktelow said her Grandfather, **Mr Caesar Bourne** and her **Aunt Bessie Pope** saw the ghost of the **monk** many times. They lived at the first house under the **Landgate Arch,** adjoining **Turkey Cock Lane**.

Whenever they saw the monk, he was 'cut off' at the knees. She said they always explained it this way - that the level of the road was lower when the monk had lived.

Kirsty Stotter told us, "I was thirteen years old and, one night, about 11 o'clock, me and a few mates were walking down **Turkey Cock Lane** when suddenly **a monk** came out of the wall. He was saying something, but I couldn't quite catch what he was saying. I think he was calling out "Daisy". I was so shocked that, as soon as it went past, I slowly walked off. As I got to the end of the lane, some one touched me on the shoulder, so I looked back. The monk was waving goodbye as he walked back into the wall. I knew it wasn't my mates, as they were in front of me!"

One night, a girl aged 13, was walking home on **Turkey Cock Lane.** Suddenly the wall bricks started shaking alongside her and **eight monks** walked out of the wall. She screamed and tried to run away - but she wasn't moving, because something was holding her around the throat. She screamed again and then ran off.

This account was recorded by **Gemma Barker, Rebecca Edwards, Dale Goldsmith, and Matthew Williams**.

CONDUIT HILL

Others have seen the **same figure** in the **chapel garden**, once the Cloisters, off **Conduit Hill** and, some 40 years ago **seven 'hooded' ghosts** were reported gliding across the grass of the garden towards the encircling brick wall. This is now a car park for the Pottery. In 1939 a section was converted to an air raid shelter and, during the excavations for the foundations, part of the original floor of the monastery crypt was revealed. But an unsolved mystery arose, for a number of skeletons were also discovered, all in a kneeling position. Perhaps the men had been praying, but what had caused their death no-one was able to discover. *[More skeletons were found in the floor of main building in 1992. Ed.]*

Mrs Chris Laverton was working at the **Hotel** which backs onto **the Monastery,** then known as The Saltings. She was looking out of the kitchen window at the back, into the car park, when she saw the **reflection of a monk** in one of the car windows. On looking more closely, it was the top half of a monk, and he looked like a dwarf - she ran away. She is convinced that it was there!! Some days later, the owner said that the car park had been infilled about three feet to make it level, <u>just</u> where Chris had seen the ghost. This would explain the **'half' man.**

The Monk has also been seen near :-

THE LANDGATE

Mrs Emily Clark, great grandmother of Mrs Amy Breeds, used to live at **23 Tower Street,** just across the road from the Landgate, with her daughter Mrs Leggatt. In 1963 she looked out of her bedroom window and saw **the Monk** in a white habit, under the **lamp-post by the Landgate.** Some people coming out of the Queen's Head also saw the Monk at that time and reported it.

HILDER'S CLIFF

At Easter 1952, **Miss Marjorie Pellers,** when staying adjoining the Tower House, on **Hilder's Cliff,** where the monk's lover once lived, saw the figure of a **cowled monk** with a sad face, who looked ill, dressed in a brown habit 'standing' by the wall of the next door property. She had no knowledge of the history of the site, or of the love story, and it was her first visit to Rye.

HIGH STREET

The **Monastery Guest House** which faces the **High Street**, but which includes some of the buildings of the Monastery, has had many sightings. **Mr Gerald Young** records how the **door bell** often rang at

2am, but only on two occasions, one in 1959 and the other in 1960, was someone there. At those times a **"foggy apparition** of the head and shoulders of a monk with a raw face" was seen. **Brother Cantator continues to frequent the area.**

LANDGATE

A lady who works at the College told us that her family had lived in **Landgate Square** when she was small. Her Mother used to see, quite regularly, **an old lady** in a long black dress and a shawl walk from the railway side of the Square and come to the pump in the centre. She would then just fade away. "Mother was never frightened of her," she said. Our informant did not know that there used to be an Almshouse, dating back to 1551, where the railway now is. It was demolished to allow the railway to be built. Perhaps it was a lady from that building?.

Mr Dick Wright said that a lady who worked at Leasam, when it was the Thomas Peacocke Boarding House, told him that she was brought up in **the Landgate**. A **'headless ghost'** was almost a member of her family. She was used to seeing it appear throughout her childhood.

FISHMARKET ROAD

Paul Byrne told us about the friend of his family who, whilst working late in **Skinner's Garage,** in order to get an urgent job done, looked up to get some tools, and saw **two feet** under the car. Thinking someone had broken in, he tried to look more closely, but there was just the faint **silhouette** of a person. It then just faded away.

NEW ROAD

Lucy Couves wrote, "One day I was walking along **New Road** and **a man** was in the middle of the road. I told him to get off it, and I carried on walking. I went past him and then looked back, but he was not there, so I ran home. The next day I was walking along the same road and he was there again. I walked past him and looked back again, but once more, he'd gone. I ran home and told my Mum and she said that there was a car crash and a man had died there - whenever I walk down that same old road, the man may be there."

Lucy Cordeux told the story that many, many pupils of **Rye Primary School** have told over the years. "At **Freda Gardham**, it is believed that **Mrs Freda Gardham** and **her dog** haunt the School. A few people have heard a dog barking and there is a picture of her and her eyes move!" **William Kirkham** said "She was always supposed to be under the stage!"

MILITARY ROAD

Gemma Barker said "My friend told me that, whilst her Mum was sleeping in a mansion house on **Military Road, a ghost** pushed her head against a pillow and tried to suffocate her. Whilst this was happening, her Mum woke up and tried to fight it off. She struggled and got her head up and saw the ghost's face. It was really weird. She said it had no eyes, nose or mouth, just hair and an empty face.

My cousin, when she was about five, had **two best friends** who were ghosts. They were friendly ghosts and went everywhere with her. One day she took them to my Dad's and accidentally left them there. My Dad suddenly felt all creepy and then he realised there were ghosts in the house, so he phoned my cousin's house and told her and her Mum to come and get them!"

DEADMAN'S LANE

We were told by a person driving from Iden to Rye, that as they were going slowly along **Deadman's Lane,** they saw **a pedestrian**. He did not move to one side as usually happens, so the driver sounded his horn. The walker just faded away slowly in the headlights and the motorist said he accelerated <u>very</u> fast to get into **The Grove** as soon as possible.

Places where Ghosts or presences have seen in Rye

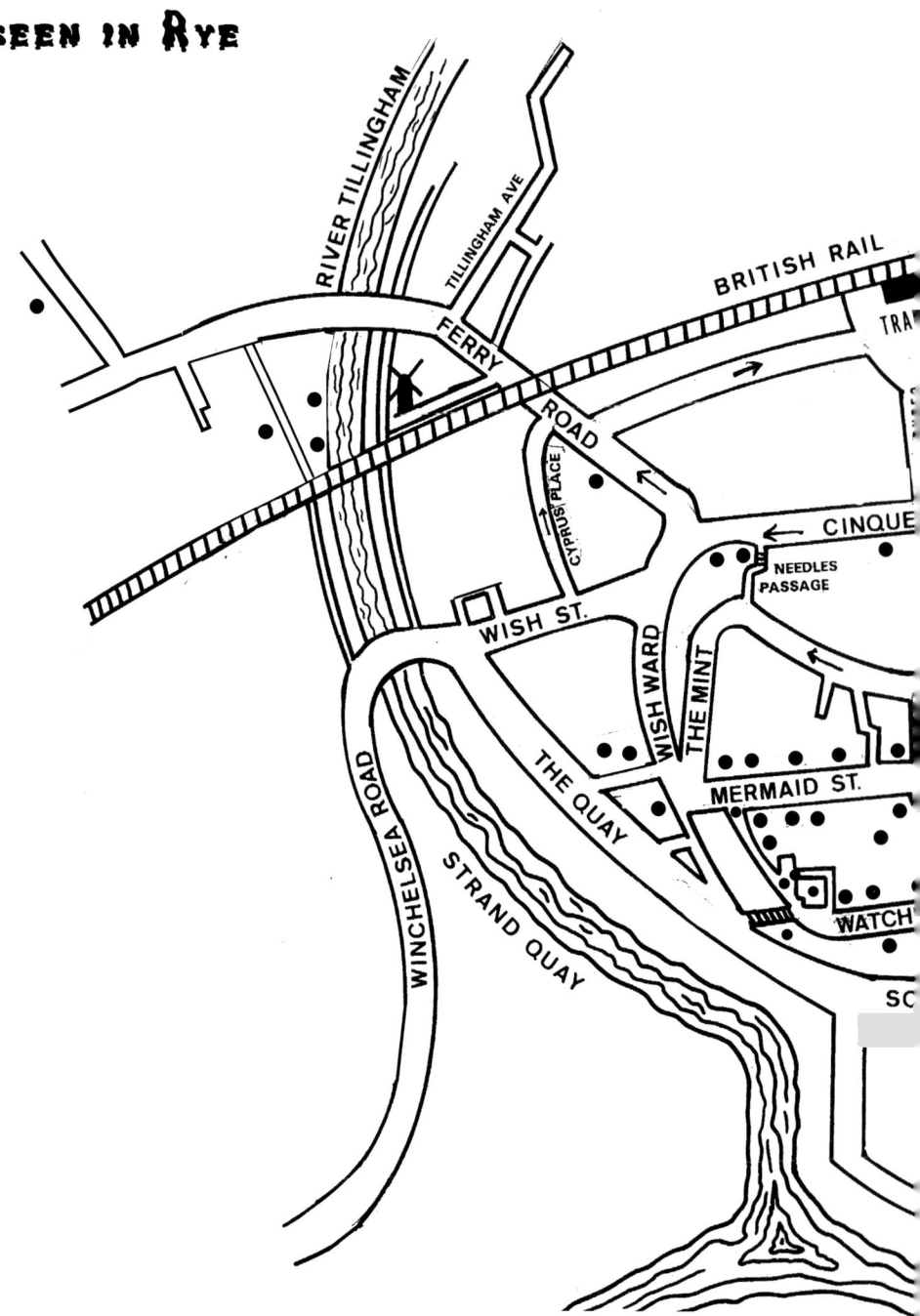

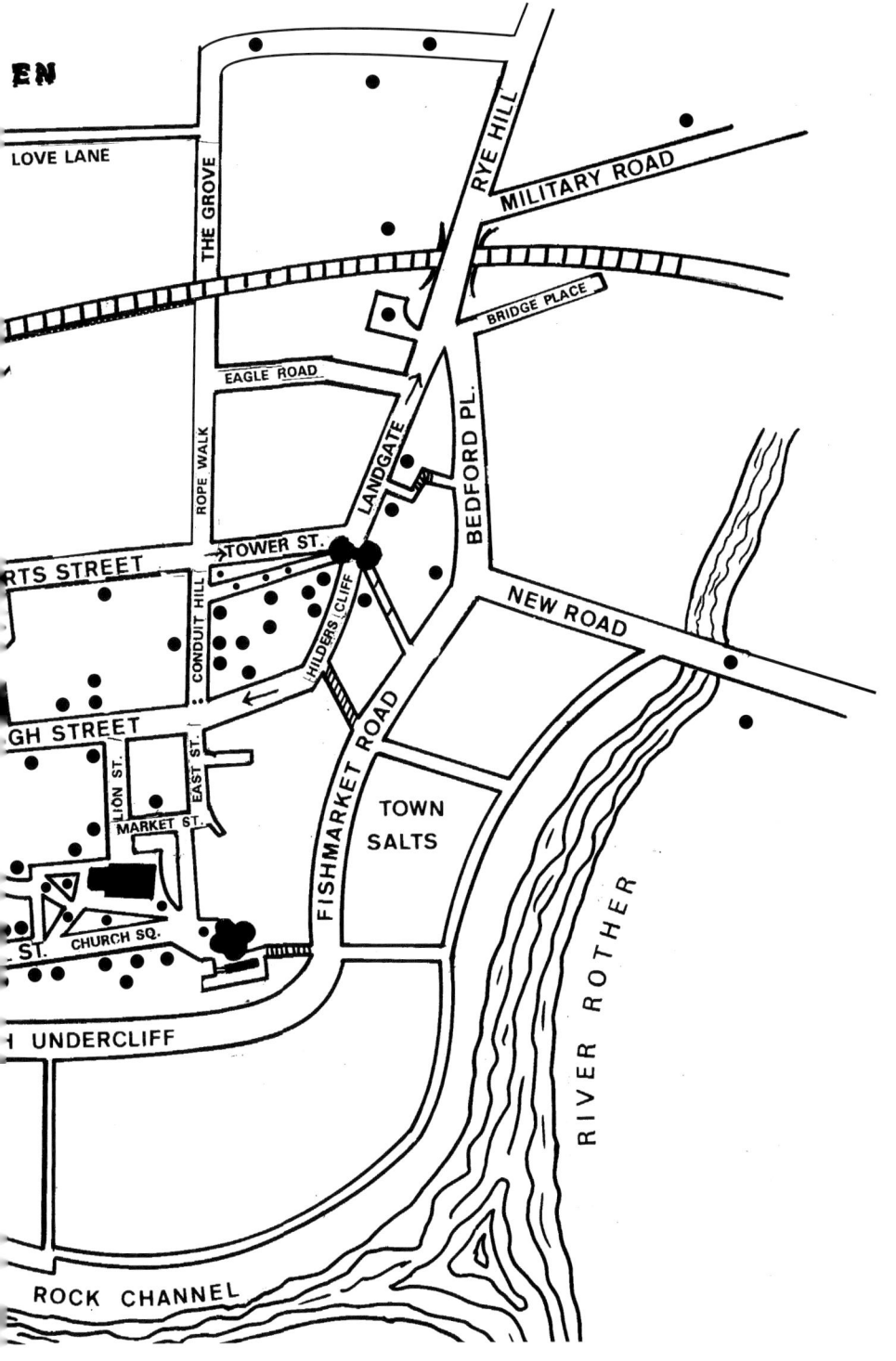

Leanne Tugwell said "Me and my Mum and my cousin Elaine, were going down **Deadman's Lane** when, on the radio, a man said 'Beware, do not look behind!' My cousin turned round and said 'Look, it's really weird!' and I said 'No!' But I did look and standing there was **a lady with a big flowery hat** and I could see through her. I asked Mum to stop and she told me to stop being silly and to sit down! But **we did see her!"**

From *"A Chronicle of Rye" by L.Grant :-*

"I have heard of a creature which answers to the **Water Kelpie** having been seen in Rye.

The story of it was told me by an old woman, and afterwards corroborated independently by her sister, who lived elsewhere and did not know that I had already heard it. Her parents, when courting, went out for a walk one evening with a dog. They were in a field when **a strange creature like a horse** came galloping past them. It had the face of a man and great eyes like saucers. The thunder of the galloping animal seemed to shake the earth. The young man tried to send the dog after it, but he was terrified and would not go. Nothing would induce him to stir. So the young man, leaving the girl, himself followed the creature, when it jumped a high fence and went paddling down into a large deep pool just below **Mountsfield.** The Kelpie is a sly devil, he roars before a loss at sea and frightens both old and young upon the shore."

CINQUE PORTS STREET

Mrs Pat Ciccone said that **Mrs Rosalind Webb** told her the story of either her Aunt or Mother being very ill in some cottages which used to stand near where the **car park** now is, **opposite the Police Station in Cinque Ports Street**. **Mrs Webb** visited her and was going to fetch something from elsewhere in the house "Don't bother, the nun is going to get it! The nun has been in to see me" the old lady said. Of course, there was no nun.

Mr John Ciccone told us that a regular customer to his shop, **opposite to the Post Office,** would come into the shop and say 'You have had someone in last night!' She could sense **'presences'**!

Mrs Hodgson told us she used to live in a shop on **Cinque Ports Street** when she was a girl. "We used to have an elderly neighbour called Mrs Sherwood who used to come round for a cup of tea with my Mother in the evenings. Our bedroom was above the dining room and we used to frighten them by leaning out of our window and touching their window with a stick. My sister Connie was a real tease - she would dress up in a sheet and pretend to be a ghost.

Our house, however, was **really ghostly.** I always felt uneasy and it felt weird - I always used to run down the passage from the toilet at one end to my bedroom at the other end, and I only felt safe when I was in my bedroom and had shut my door. My Father used to shout up "What's the matter? Is he after you tonight?" It was the same in later life also. I still didn't like it and I can remember asking my husband to walk down the passage with me.

My Mother saw "**a lady**" several times and one day she said she was **a lady in grey**, in old fashioned clothes."

FERRY ROAD

Mrs Gladys Mann told us that every night between 20 to 10 and 10 o'clock, there would be a series of **bangs** 'in' her sitting room wall. This series of hard taps would go on and on and they nick-named him/it 'George'. There was nobody in the houses on either side of hers. All her family and friends heard it - it went on through Christmas celebrations, indeed it went on for years. In the end, two years ago, thoroughly exasperated, she shouted "For God's sake George, Go!" They have never heard him again! Often there would be **a smell** of cooking bacon and eggs with the sounds, and although there has been no noise since, the smell of cooking occasionally occurs.
NB. Mrs Mann told us that two weeks ago, (November 1995), she woke up from a nap in the lounge to see the figure of **an old man** in the space under the stairs, on the opposite side of the room from where she was lying. He had a shock of grey hair and wore a raincoat. She immediately thought "George!" As she watched he just faded away!! She had never **seen** him before.

A strange story about the same house was told us by **Mr Bill Cutting**, who sadly died last year. He used to live with his family in the same house in **Ferry Road** during the First World War and he said "I remember when I was about nine, my Father was doing some work in the sitting room and he found a trap door, which led to a passage between the kitchen and the sitting room, downwards. We went along it until his candle went out. We wondered if it was a smugglers passage?"

(See RYE MEMORIES VOL. 8 RECOLLECTIONS OF WILLIAM CUTTING)

It was **this wall** which had the banging sounds in recent years and from which 'George' appeared!!

THE NEEDLES PASSAGE

In response to our request for Ghost Stories, we were told by one gentleman, about the time that he was taking the short cut from Cinque Ports Street to The Mint through the **Needles Passage**, very late one night. He became aware of someone coming towards him. He heard the **footsteps** and, as he turned the bend in the middle of the passage, he prepared to stand to one side to allow the person to pass. However the steps passed him, and then died away going towards Cinque Ports Street, but there was no-one there to see! He said he was petrified.

HIGH STREET

Mrs Hodgson used to work in a dress shop on the **High Street** and she told us :-

"I was in the stock room with two girls when one of them exclaimed "What was that? Something pushed past me!" The air was **icy cold** and I felt rooted to the floor. Another person who lived at this property years ago, had, on occasions, seen the vision of **a small boy.**"

She continued "In another shop I know of on the **High Street**, the occupants have had vases, a bedside table and various other **objects, moved** from one part of the room to another during the night."

At the **White Vine Hotel** on **the High Street**, a couple, on being asked at breakfast if they had slept well, said "Well, not really, '**someone**' was in our room. Something was definitely there. It was quite a pleasant 'presence'." This was told to the Editor in November 1995, and **Mrs Geraldine Bromley,** the owner, confirmed the account. She added "The two people concerned were very responsible people - one associated with Canterbury Cathedral and the other with Lincoln Cathedral. She said that she was changing the linen in that same bedroom and put two **pillow cases** on the bed. She turned round to get a sheet, and one pillow case was back on the chair!

She believes **the 'presence'** is a child and is mischievous, but with a nice feel to it. **Mrs Bromley** said "The kitchen is a favourite place for the 'happenings'. Three carrots were put in with the onions, sugar was discovered in the potatoes and five plastic container lids were found in the flour sack. Today a mixing bowl is missing. All these things have happened this week!" (November 13th 1995)

Mrs Heather Sutton, for her lunch break at **Horrell's Chemists**, went into the back garden, belonging to Mrs Linda Hawthorne. She became aware that someone was watching her. The next day the same happened. She looked up and saw **a monk** in a brown habit in the corner opposite to her. She has seen him on two occasions. She thought he was 'vetting' her, but she felt quite comfortable and mentally told him she was doing no harm.

TILLING GREEN SCHOOL

Mrs Cicely Prebble works at **Tilling Green School.** Twice within a few weeks last year, early in the morning, before it got light, she was aware of a '**presence**' in the Staff Room. The second time, in particular, she was very frightened. There was a toy animal on the window sill, and its movable head was shaking!

She wondered if it had anything to do with the young man who fell through the roof and was killed a few years ago.

ON GIBBET'S MARSH

In January 1993, **a colleague** of the Editor's, was taking his dog for a walk across **Gibbet's Marsh** at about 12.45am. As he approached the kissing-gate by the River Tillingham and the railway, but about 30 yards away, the dog stopped dead. It would not move. A figure of **a man** dressed in a long raincoat and with a trilby hat on, as in the 1940's, appeared. He encouraged the dog to move and, as they moved, the man slowly faded away!!

Dale Goldsmith said "I was walking back home one day, from a club, which I used to go to, when I decided to go through **Gibbet's Marsh,** instead of going around town. I opened one gate, but it shut, then a **cold gust of wind** hit me. I carried on walking and opened the next gate. This shut too and then opened again. I looked back and I saw nothing then, but gradually I saw the outline of **a shepherd** was coming towards me. I ran all the way home; nobody will believe me!"

Jamie Haffenden told us "Early one morning, about 2.30am, my Dad was walking to work over **Gibbet's Marsh,** when he looked up and saw a **shepherd,** who had a sort of old smock on like they used to wear. There was a ground mist at the time which came up to his waist so my Dad couldn't see what he was wearing below."

THE MARSHES AROUND RYE

During the **Great War** a sad incident occurred. A man named **Axell** was affected every month by the full moon - literally a 'lunatic'. His usual habit was to go to **the fields between Rye and Camber Castle** on those nights and dance naked in the moonlight. A soldier on sentry duty on those marshes in the First War challenged the **man/ghost** he saw in the eerie moonlight. Of course Mr Axell did not know the password and didn't answer. The soldier was terrified and shot Mr Axell dead.

Mrs Hodgson told us her father had seen a **'vision'** one day when he was going down **Rye Harbour Road** in the days when it was full of pot-holes. It was so powerful the it changed his life and he became very religious after that.

OTHER RYE GHOST STORIES

Sarah Benn said "In **Rye**, one of my sister's friends has lots of **posters**. One day she went into her room and all her posters had been taken down and were put on her bed neatly. She ran downstairs to ask if anyone had put her posters on her bed. BUT NOBODY HAD!"

Melissa Field said "There was a Bed & Breakfast **near Rye** and this girl was staying with her sister who owned it. There were three floors, the bottom floor was where the residents ate their breakfast, the middle floor was where they slept and, on the top floor, there were a couple of spare rooms. The sister was sleeping on the middle floor, and as there was no room for the girl, she had to sleep on the top floor. Half way through the night, the girl woke up and heard **crying**. In the morning she asked her sister about it, but she said there was no-one with a child staying there. That night, the girl and her sister stayed up on the top floor and they both heard crying. The next day she phoned the person who used to own the B&B. He said that some years before, a woman used to beat her child and one day they found the girl lying in the corner of a room on the top floor, dead, her mother had killed her."

Taken from *"A Chronicle of Rye"* :-

"Related to me by a friend who happened to be staying there (in Rye). She and her husband were in bed, in separate beds. The husband was asleep, when she saw **the figure of a man** standing at the foot of hers. He had long hair reaching his shoulders and was dressed in a close-fitting coat or habit fastened up to the throat. His hands were crossed over his breast and he had the most worried expression upon his face.

She looked at him for a minute, then, feeling uncomfortable about it, called to her husband. 'Light the candle quickly, Harry!' He awoke and did so and the figure disappeared.

The lady happened to be an artist, and, in the morning, she drew a pencil sketch from memory of the apparition, which she showed me afterwards. The face had such a strangely haunted expression that I could scarcely bear to look at it."

Gina Matthews wrote "A man called **Robert Peake** who lives in **Rye**, was walking home from work, when suddenly, **a tall man with a long black cloak and a top hat,** came walking past him very fast, as if he was in a rush. As the man went round the corner, Robert followed him but the man was nowhere to be seen. Lots of other people have seen the man around Rye."

★

STORIES FROM THE AREA AROUND RYE

APPLEDORE

Mrs Julie Fowle said that a **smell of Vanilla** used to appear suddenly in their house in **Appledore**. The family used to think it meant a 'presence' had come in.

ASHFORD

Bethany Wilson wrote "When I was three, we lived in **Ashford** and every night about eight, I would see an **old man**. He was quite small and wore a black hat, black gloves, black cloak and waistcoat, black trousers and he had a black walking stick. I told Mum and she came in and told him to go away. He didn't and so she told him again, and he did go then. I haven't seen him since, also we have moved!"

BECKLEY

Lucy Still said they had a 'horrible ghost' in their **barn** when she was about two years old. The atmosphere was **freezing cold** and her parents had it exorcised. It is perfectly all right now.

Laura Bowler and Zoe Whiting told us that they had both heard of the following ghost. "In **Beckley** there is a pub called the **Royal Oak,** which in Victorian times used to be the local Workhouse. The ghost seen there is **a lady** dressed in blue and at about 10.30pm she comes down, wanders around, moves stuff and mumbles something you can not pick out. She seems to go back upstairs when the pub closes. She has been seen twice, both times at Hallowe'en and the day after."

Donna Power told us that "Before we moved into our house at **Beckley**, a man and woman called Mr and Mrs Ladd used to live there. After his wife died of cancer, he became ill and had to go into a home. He was aged 89. That is when we moved in. We met him and became quite good friends and he left us his cat as he couldn't look after it any more. He used to come to our house to visit his cat and us when he was feeling better. He really did love the house.

One night my Mum got out of the bath, got dressed and came out of the bathroom. My Dad was at the top of the stairs and was talking to her. Mum could hear Dad, but she couldn't see him - it was as if there was **a big white blob** in front of him and it moved a little from side to side and up and down. Mum couldn't believe it, and then, about ten minutes later there was a phone call to say Mr Ladd had died ten minutes ago!!

BIDDENDEN

ZENA PIGGOTT'S STORY- told to the Group in 1988.
[In RYE MEMORIES VOLUME 8].

"In 1970, my Father went to stay with an old school friend, Tony, who lived in a small cottage in the grounds of a large house in **Biddenden.** It was November. When my Father and Tony got talking, Tony told of how, back in the last year, he had a most strange experience. He had gone to bed and been awakened by the sound of drums. On going out to investigate, he found nothing, but he could hear the crunching of gravel and chanting, as if some sort of procession was coming up the drive, only no one was visible.

My Father was fascinated but thought no more about it. It wasn't until the third night of his stay he considered looking into the strange noises. On this night my Father recalls watching TV with Tony. It was a film and so, when the sound of drums were heard, my father thought nothing of it, but Tony did! "He went as white as a sheet!" said my Father. Tony turned the TV off and asked my father to listen. He did - and he heard the **chanting and the crunching of gravel.** He looked out the window, but saw nothing! 'It was the first time I have ever been scared, really scared!', my Father said to me. Tony and my Father did not sleep that night!!

Next morning, they took a trip to the local Library. They found out that, in the early 1800's, the man occupying the big house murdered his family and was hanged for it. The procession my Father and Tony heard was, in fact, the "hanging march" of the murderer!"

BREDE
THE GHOST OF BREDE PLACE

Spencer Fielding told us that, when he lived in **Brede Place**, he often was woken in the night by **bells** ringing in the cellars.

He said his father, **Mr Fielding**, saw a ghost of **a monk** above the flames, when **Brede Place** had a serious fire and burned in the 1970's.

Mr Clifford Bloomfield says "In April 1941 I left the Post Office and took what I considered to be a better job with the then local land drainage authority. I spent my time working with three surveyors, but at one time with **Miss D.V.Harding.** My impression was that she was of private means and did not really need a job, but did something she chose to do rather than something to which she was directed, as could happen in war time. We spent many an hour during her early weeks with us looking for a house to buy. She was looking for an olde worlde country house - and there was a big choice.

One particular day we had been to an excavator working in the Brede Valley. The driver suggested she took a look at **Brede Place** as he knew it was empty - I think he now spoke with his tongue in his cheek! Driving in its direction, we stopped to ask the way, and we were told we should first find **Miss Claire Sheridan.** We did not know it at the time, but she was a cousin of **Winston Churchill.** On entering her drive, we found the grounds full of all manner of carvings, idols and tall totem poles. Miss Harding was not a person to be put off and up to the front door she went. She said to Miss Sheridan 'I understand **Brede Place** is empty and do you think the owner would be interested in selling it?' Miss Sheridan laughed 'I should not think so — it's been the family home for 200 years! But you're welcome to look it over. The Canadian Army has only just vacated it and if you look round the grounds you will find the gardener.'

This we did - he was an old man, working on a ladder, clipping a yew tree. We told him of Miss Sheridan's permission and he went to the summer house to get the key. It was so large it had to be carried by the shank. The two of us walked up to the front door which had a Gothic arch. We turned the key easily, pushed open the door, entered the hall and then wandered the corridors and rooms, upstairs and downstairs until we came to a lower room. On opening the door, we saw it was a small chapel within the house. Taking a cursory look around, we left, closing the door, and passed into a small hall with another flight of stairs. About to continue along another corridor, we both stopped for some unaccountable reason. I looked back, and, in the closed doorway, **a misty figure** emerged. I looked in disbelief - we were both transfixed as it moved across the hall before us and ascended the stairs and went out of sight.

We hurriedly left the house, locked the door, returned the key to the summer house and got into the car. It was only then, and as we were leaving, that we were able to relax and exchange our experiences. I have rarely mentioned this to anyone. I still don't think I believe in ghosts, or do I? Recently I was in the company of **Mr Layton Frewen** of Northiam. He was interested and said the precise location where we had seen the ghost was known to his family."

[Extract from RYE MEMORIES VOL. 14 : WINGS OVER RYE, Memories of Clifford Bloomfield.]

Gregory Coleman in *[RYE MEMORIES :VOL. 15 : BYGONE BROAD OAK AND BREDE],* wrote :-

"**Brede Place** is reputed to be haunted by several ghosts, including an old lady, a ghost priest called Father John, two men fighting with swords in a bedroom and the ghost of Ralph Oxenbridge. A physic woman called Shirley tried to contact the **Oxenbridge ghost**. He tried to entice her to leave her body, saying it would be far easier to converse when she left her shell. The spell was broken by making the sign of the Cross, but this was not before she had an insight into the ghost's violent death. She saw Ralph asleep and then a man in black creep into the room with a sword, which he plunged into the sleeping man's chest.

It is known that the Oxenbridge's had a long standing feud with their neighbours, the Cheyney's of Snailham, over a boundary dispute. The Oxenbridge reaction to this murderous outrage was to burn down the Cheyney's house and kill the murderer.

Lady Randolph Churchill visited her sister, **Mrs Frewen** at **Brede Place,** (their maiden name was Jerome and they were from New York). She was put into the haunted room, but she did not enjoy the experience and refused to visit Brede again.

Sir Winston Churchill occupied the same room on another occasion and slept undisturbed.

This ghost is of **a lady** who died suddenly and tragically in that room about 200 years ago, although no-one seems to know the exact circumstances. In May 1953 a fifteen year old schoolboy saw the ghost at 2am and she was wearing a dress with high shoulders and a long full skirt.

Part of **the grounds** is also haunted. **Claire Sheridan** (the daughter of Mr and Mrs Morton Frewen), used to be aware of it on the hill at the back of the house, in the dell and at the upper gate. Sometimes at dusk she would feel as though someone was trying to push her away from the woods. She and her friend Shirley (the psychic), tried to find out who was haunting the dell. As related by them, **the ghost is that of a young girl** called Martha who was raised at Brede from childhood and became a servant at **Brede Place**, during the reign of Henry VIII. Martha thinks of herself as a very wicked woman as she allowed the two sons of the house to use her body and she also stole lots of things. Her one good memory is of her love for the Woodsman and their times together in the dell. It was on his account she stole her lady's jewels. There was a tremendous uproar in the house when the loss of the jewels was discovered. Meanwhile the Woodsman had run off with the jewels, leaving Martha to take the blame by herself. At this time she was pregnant by one of the two sons. The lady of the house paid some men to drag Martha up the hill where she was hanged on a tree overlooking the dell. Afterwards they burnt her body with the garden rubbish. Martha believed she was wicked but liked to stay in the dell where she and her lover had once been happy and make sure nobody chopped the trees down - which she was very concerned about!

Mrs Janet Pollard confirmed to us that Claire Sheridan used to talk frequently to the Maid who was hanged.

GROANING BRIDGE, BREDE

'**The Ogre of Brede**' was also known as '**Old Oxenbridge**'. He is reputed to have liked the flesh of children and enjoyed one for his meal every night. The children of Brede decided to do something about it. They agreed to get him drunk and then, when he was unconscious, cut him in half with a wooden saw. This occurred in **Stubb's Lane** by the **Groaning Bridge,** between Brede Place and the Church. This bridge is said to be haunted and generations of Brede children have been frightened of passing over it.

It is not quite certain which member of the Oxenbridge family the legend is about, but the likely one was Sir Goddard Oxenbridge, who lived in the sixteenth century. However, that man seems to have been a kindly man and a devout Christian. The legend of the giant seems to have been used by smugglers to frighten villagers away from their activities.

This story was told us by many people including **Hannah Brown, Gregory Coleman, Janet Pollard and Mrs Masters.**

BREDE CHURCH

Mrs Janet Pollard's father was the Churchwarden at Brede for many years and one day, he was about to lock up the **Church,** when he noticed **a man in an old fashioned suit,** a stove pipe hat and buckled shoes sat on a chair under the tower. He asked him what he was doing there, and he just faded away.

Brede Church has many **'presences'** and people have been aware of 'someone' else being present on may occasions.

Several people told us that **a white lady** has been seen in **Brede Churchyard**.

In the **Churchyard** there is a plain oak cross alongside the wall next to the adjoining house, with **'Damaris'** carved on it. Damaris Richardson fell in love with Lewis Smith who lived in the large house next door to the Church. Unfortunately they were of different social class and his parents thought she was 'below' him and would not allow them to marry. The lovers used to meet at the spot where the cross is now. It marks too, where she was buried after dying of a broken heart at the age of only twenty two years. Lewis Smith never married and died, aged 65, on February 23 1896. Is she the white lady? She is supposed to re-visit her lover's home and there is one report of her being seen in a bedroom of the house next door.

BROAD OAK

David Adams wrote "I did not used to believe, but after my Nan died about five years ago, I started to do so. She used to live with us in our house in **Broad Oak**, until she died in one of the rooms. Ever after, it was nearly always very cold in her room, and you often thought you had seen something there in the evenings."

Mrs Louise Whiteman told us that this happened at her home in **Broad Oak** in 1992. "On the afternoon of August 19th, our dog had to be put down. She was twelve years old and had suffered from cancer of the spine for some months. As you can imagine, the whole family was very upset and our two bedroomed bungalow suddenly seemed very empty. The dog had a special place she liked to settle in our house. It was in the hallway where she could see into both the living room and my bedroom, where my husband has a corner set up as an office, for in this way she could see both of us.

During the evening I was sitting in the living room and I happened to glance towards the hallway out of habit. I was extremely surprised to see **the dog** lying in her usual place in the hall. She looked younger and happy and not in any pain at all. It was as if she had come back to say she was alright and we needn't worry about her. This was the only time it happened.

BROOKLAND

Karen Fuller told us "My Dad's cousin Rita and her friend were cleaning at the **School in Brookland**. They had just finished and were walking past the toilets, when all **this smoke** came from inside. They looked inside but no-one was there. They had locked the main entrance door behind them as they came in, so they checked to see if anyone had broken in. They didn't find anyone anywhere and the next day they told the headmaster about it. He said that a cleaner had hung herself in the toilets and that she had been a very heavy smoker. Lots of other people had seen the smoke coming out of there at separate times.

CAMBER

Carrie Ann Catho said "My Mum cleans for a lady who has a big white house in **Camber** called the Watchhouse, which is next to the sea. Her husband had cancer and because he didn't want to live in the condition he was in, he shot himself in a pink bedroom at the front of the house. After cleaning there, Mum goes home and then, when she goes back the next week, sometimes things have been **moved around** or thrown onto the carpet. When I go into the room it always feels cold and as if someone is watching me. It might be my imagination.

My Mum was coming back home about 11 pm and she saw **a figure** walking towards her on the other side of the road, the **Lydd-Camber Road by Johnson's Field**. As it got nearer, she realised it was walking about a foot in the air. She looked more closely and saw it was a monk, dressed in a brown habit. It walked about another five metres and then disappeared. She has seen it in another place and knows someone else who has seen it."

EAST GULDEFORD

Mrs Doris Carree told us. 'During the 1980's my husband was a shepherd on **Romney Marsh** and we lived at **East Guldeford**. The sheep were housed in lambing sheds at lambing time. He used to pay a last visit to look at them in the late evening about 11 -12 o'clock midnight, and I quite often went with him.

On one occasion we came out of **Salts Farmhouse** to walk to the farm, **(Salts Farm)**, when, across the road immediately in front of us, came **a man** in what looked like a long black cloak or coat. I believe Len said "Good evening" but got no reply. The footpath from our house to the farm is about 100 yards long and the man walked just in front of us all the way. I must admit I felt a bit scary as we came to the end of the path to cross the main road. I thought "Now, I wonder where he is going now?" As you can guess, down there in the Marsh, one sees very few people walking at that time of night. However, he just disappeared into nowhere. It certainly was a strange feeling!'

Mr Rob. Charman used to live at the **corner of the Camber Road**, at **East Guldeford.** He told us that he saw **a man** at the foot of his bed, several times, which then disappeared.

He also told us that he and some friends were climbing over the gate towards **East Guldeford Church** one day, when they saw a **'blazing halo of fire'** around the Church. He turned to shout to the rest of his mates and when he turned back, it had gone.

EWHURST

PADGEM FARM

Padgem Farm is owned by an ex-insurance broker who has now turned his hand to egg production. The house he received with the farm is plagued with a single nuisance, **the ghost** of Mrs Vincent, who seems to appear between May and August. John, the present owner, is not the only one to notice that the last owners of the house put this as one of the major reasons for them leaving.

John says that the ghost appears as a little girl in Victorian dress or a woman dressed in a fairy suit and it has been seen as a ten inch fairy who dances on the patio. This may seem amazing, but we see no reason to disbelieve him, as he himself was a disbeliever <u>until it happened to him.</u>

The ghost in question has been seen many times, but only by men. The aftermath of the ghosts antics have been seen by others however - things like cutlery strewn all over the floor and metal tags pulled off the Aga in the kitchen.

John now refuses to stay in the house on his own, as the last time he did, when his family went to the USA, he had a very frightening experience. Whilst in bed, he heard an almighty crash from the kitchen, similar to that when all the cutlery was suddenly dropped on the floor. When he checked there was nothing there.

He also recalls several times when he has been sat watching television and a little girl in Victorian dress has run past him and hidden behind the curtain. On inspecting the curtain he found nothing.

He has also heard **knocks** on the door, gone to answer it, to find the ghost standing there, but, then, it suddenly vanishes. Due to the evidence given, we believe this to be a genuine ghost.

THE WHITE DOG INN

This inn is set in one of the few places to have escaped the all seeing eye of property developers. Ewhurst is possibly one of the most beautiful villages in the county. It has very few amenities, but the one it does have is the pub.

The White Dog is set on the top of the valley side overlooking Bodiam Castle and dates back to 1576. Over the years it has had many owners, but the present occupiers have only been there since May 1994. The landlord, **Mick Jones,** has experienced occurrences he cannot explain and therefore believes the pub to be haunted. This theory can be backed up by many of the regulars, some of whom we spoke to.

He told us that some nights he could be all alone in the bar and hear **footsteps** going across the top of him, from the top of the stairs on the second floor to the room where the pub used to end, and then just stop. After hearing this several times, Mick checked all the rooms in the pub and any place where a person could possibly hide, but he found nobody.

He also told us about the **tankards** that are hung on strong hooks at the back of the bar. One night he, and several witnesses, saw one of the tankards, the second from the left, just fall off one of these hooks onto the surface underneath. He showed us the tankards and we agreed that it was impossible for these to fall off on their own. They could not have balanced on the hook tip.

The chef told us that the **door from the kitchen**, normally wedged open, can and does close, with the wedge still in place.
The Ewhurst incidents were recorded by Andrew Tomkins

GUESTLING

An **old lady,** dressed in white, with a pleasant smiling face, has been seen several times in a bedroom at night at **Church Farm, Guestling**.

Martine Devitt used to attend **Broomham School, Guestling**, and told us of the time when she, with four girls, two boys and a teacher saw the **ghost of an old lady** in old fashioned clothes in the Hall. It has been seen several times.

HASTINGS

Paul Byrne told us of some strange happenings in their flat when they lived in **Hastings.** "My Dad had an ash tray on a stand and it was moved many times to the opposite side of the room overnight. We also had a washing machine which would start and move to the centre of the kitchen on its own. The most frightening was the gas fire, which would suddenly shoot flames right across the lounge. We had the Gas Board out many times to investigate it, but they said there was nothing wrong. But it kept happening and so we moved back to Rye because of it."

These incidents were confirmed to us at Open Evening by Paul's Mother and Grandparents.

Mr James Davison used to own the **Cambridge Hotel in Hastings**. He said he had a regular customer called Peter who **always** dressed in a duffel coat, corduroy trousers, a grotty pullover and boots. He got married at the age of 50 and moved to Poole to live. He died five years later and he and his wife had, by then, had a son called Toby.

"The wife rang us one day, distraught, to ask if she and the boy could come to stay for a while. We agreed and they had been with us a few weeks, when my wife was upstairs one day. She came downstairs and said to me 'Peter has just come into our bedroom and said I'd to tell Marie there's nothing to worry about. It's all right.'

She described Peter being dressed in tee shirt, shorts, plimsolls and he had a bag over his shoulder. We couldn't understand the unusual clothing he was wearing, but his wife then told us how he had died. The three of them had been on the beach, when Peter had got bored and decided to go to the library for a book. He pulled on his tee shirt with his swimming shorts and plimsolls and he picked up Toby's satchel and put it over his shoulder. As he was crossing the road from the beach, he was run over and killed."

Mr Davison told us too, that a **Victorian fruit seller** passed through the Saloon Bar dozens of times.

"We also had **a little girl** of about eight years old who sat on the end of my children's beds and played with their toys at night. They saw her many times."

Martin Bryant told us, "I believe in ghosts because I think I have seen one in my Uncle's house in **Hastings**. Also my Uncle told me that when he was younger, he had **a photo** of an old lady who had died a few years ago. One day, when my Uncle tried to touch the photo, he froze still for about twenty minutes. He decided to put the photo in an envelope and send it back to the house where the old lady had lived. When Uncle got back home, from the post box, THE PHOTO WAS ON THE TABLE IN THE FRONT ROOM. My Uncle then took the photo back to the lady's house by car. The new owner of her house, also a lady, burned the photo with blessings then and there, and the ghost hasn't been seen since."

Lettie Moon said "My Nan told me that once she was sitting in her living room in **Hastings**, when she started to drift off to sleep. She woke up with a start and saw the ghost of **an old man** lingering. He slowly faded away. A few weeks later she was asleep in her bed, when she woke up, just after midnight, to see the same old man standing by the window. The next day she did some research and found out that the flats were built on the site of an old grave yard."

Robert Miller told **Mrs Surman**, "When I was up at my old pub, **(The Miller's Arms at Ore)**, there was a ghost. There was a pool table. At Christmas we had finished playing pool and had set the table up for another game. The **balls started moving by themselves**. All were potted, except the black, which was bouncing around the table. This happened afterwards every night at 10.45pm. Eventually we got rid of the pool table and put up another dart board. **Pictures** then started moving and there were shadows of no-one!

It was an old boy called Bill Wimbourne, who died playing darts. He used to push the bar staff!"

Eleanor Burnston wrote "I went to my friend's house in **Hollington** and sat in her chair in the front room, with some popcorn. We were watching a video called 'The Rocky Horror Show'. It was about 10 o'clock at night when, suddenly, a **cold gust of wind** blew around me. Maxine noticed me shivering and said 'Are you cold?' I said 'Yes, all of a sudden it went cold.' She replied 'Oh, Don't worry, that's only Sally, the ghost.' I thought 'What ghost?' Maxine said that there had been a ghost for ages.

That night we stayed up and, at exactly 3 o'clock, just like Max said, there were **footsteps** going up the stairs! The next day the **room went cold** and the dog went out yelping!"

Timothy Biggs said "In 1987 there was a bad storm. We lived in a flat with an old lady living above us. She was mad and had two cats. The storm caused the roof to collapse and she was crushed and her cats streaked out and died from starvation. I believe she died from her injuries. Ever since, whenever there's a storm, **she can be heard walking** and her **cats mewing** for food."

James Smith told Mrs Surman that, in 1889, between **Hastings** and **Tunbridge Wells**, a relation of his had something happen to him which became a true ghost story. "This middle-aged dude went around mouthing off at everybody. One day he was caught stealing bread and put in the stocks. Of course this was pure paradise for the people the middle-aged dude had mouthed off to. The shopkeeper (the one he had stolen the bread from) came up with a mouldy pumpkin, lifted it up and SPLAT!! He threw it over his head. The middle-aged dude could not breathe and he was suffocated to death. In the middle of the night, on Hallowe'en, he will haunt every house in Great Britain."

ICKLESHAM

In the 1800's there was an Irish Wake for the life of the late landlord of the **Queen's Head Inn, at Icklesham**, called John Gutsell, whilst he was lying in his coffin on the bar. **John** has been seen many times since, sat in a chair by the bar and many times there has been the **smell** of smoke from his pipe.

IDEN

The landlord and lady of the **Bell Inn** told us of four things which they couldn't explain.

One night, **mugs fell off the shelf** at one end of the bar, whilst they watched. No-one was near them.

They have two large **dogs** and on another night they rushed into their bedroom very frightened, an unheard of occurrence - one an Alsatian, the other a wolf hound.

Yet another night saw some very strong **beading come off** the wall. It had been very securely fastened.

The stables are being converted into holiday accommodation at the moment, and the workmen are sure there is '**something**' there.

Abigail Whitewick wrote "Well, there was a man and a lady in bed asleep at their house in **Iden,** when the man woke up and saw a figure at the end of the bed. It started to go to the bathroom, so the man followed. When he got there, it was gone. In the morning, when his wife woke up, she said 'Something walked over me!'"

LYDD

Mrs Yvonne Beadle told us of the time she lived with her family at the **George Hotel, Lydd.** It was an old coaching inn, with a long corridor, with guest rooms leading off it on each side, on the first floor. At that time, Yvonne was working as an air hostess flying out of Lydd Airport, and she shared a room with another hostess called Pam. Their room was on the second floor, which was laid out along a corridor, as the floor below. However, there were only two proper rooms on this floor, one at each end, and in between was a series of small 'baggage rooms' under the eaves, which had no windows, but did have doors onto the corridor.

Yvonne told us that suddenly in the middle of the night, there was a **violent shaking and rattling** in the joint walls with the baggage rooms, making the whole structure vibrate. They were terrified, looked outside their door, but there was nothing there. For a couple of weeks, all was quiet, then it happened again. This pattern kept repeating itself.

She went on "Then, one night, Pam had a 'night stop,' and I refused to sleep in the room on my own. The Hotel was full and Mother said there was nowhere else for me to go. Eventually, she agreed to sleep with me, all the time muttering under her breath, 'I've never heard such nonsense in my life. What rubbish!' We'd just settled down for the night, when the deafening banging began again. Mum was terrified, 'What's that? Oh, my God! Get Kim'. We rushed down stairs. I had an Alsatian dog called Kim who was very obedient and he had slept by my bed as a rule, but, after the first experience of the banging, he was very reluctant to go upstairs. I would pull and be left with the collar in my hand!

We then asked the Physic Research Society to come to investigate. They didn't want any details, just to search on their own. They found a **'presence'** in the guest room <u>under</u> the baggage room. After they had been, we never heard the noises again.

My sister and I had another strange experience there. One night we were woken up about 2 am by an **eerie voice** outside calling 'Robert'. Our brother's name was Robert, so we leaned out of our window, to see if we could see who was calling him, but no-one was there, and the sound kept coming - it just seemed to be floating in the air. We found out that a Robert O'Neil had been shot and killed by the Hawkhurst Gang in the yard. Perhaps it was his girl friend looking for him?

Neither Mum, nor Jennifer, nor the chambermaid ever wanted to go upstairs on their own."

NEW ROMNEY

Kay Payton wrote "I don't know if ghosts are real or not, but from my point of view, I've been in an old house in **New Romney** with a friend. It is really spooky, and has been boarded up by the Council, because a man hanged himself in there. From then, no-one has gone in to live, because they believe it is haunted."

NORTHIAM

Hayley Mash, who lives at the **Crown and Thistle,** told us that there have been several ghosts sighted there.

She has seen **a woman**, aged about forty, in old fashioned clothes of a long dress and a bonnet, walk through the side of the building. She saw her for the first time last Christmas.

Her Mother has seen **a man** upstairs in doublet and hose with a feather in his hat. Her brother's friend **Geoff**. has also seen this apparition. **Brian**, who looks after the pub when the family are away, has also seen the 'man in padded shorts'. He has also **seen a man and a woman**, arm in arm, on the stairs. In November 1995, he saw the same woman standing by his bed, staring at him.

The Hayes Arms Hotel has a ghost. In the 1700's, a lady staying in the hotel, visited Captain Saunters room and was murdered there. Since then, **rooms go hot and cold** suddenly and **pictures** are taken off the walls and are left on the floor, leaning against the wall. One corridor is always cold. I felt this in this very hot summer.

Thanks to John, Carol, Graeme, Mick, Sue and the Bar staff and employees of the Hayes Arms Hotel, Northiam.   *Andrew Tomkins*

PETT

Rosie Head told us that, in their house in **Pett,** her Mother had heard '**things' going** upstairs. Her sister had seen an **old lady** in a rocking chair, which, to other family members, was just rocking on its own! She told Rosie that the lady read her stories at bedtime, but no-one else had seen or heard her.

RUCKINGE

Andrea Loring said that "this happened in **Ruckinge** to one of my friends called **Sophie Batt.** She was talking to her Mum who was standing at the bottom of the stairs about six feet away from her. Suddenly a **match box** just flew out of no-where and Sophie and her Mum were the only people in the house. Spooky!!"

RYE FOREIGN

Mr Fairbrother told us that when he was working as a milkman and delivering along **Leasam Lane**, he heard someone behind him. At first he thought it was a cow on the other side of the hedge, but he plucked up courage and looked and there was nothing there. It happened several times and he was so disturbed by it that he soon gave up his job.

Sophie Lehane said that "When **Gina Matthews** was younger, at night, when she was going to sleep, she saw the **shadow of a man** at the door and she thought it was her Dad. It happened every night and she would run to the door, but 'it' would be gone.

One day her friend went to her house to play and they were up in a room when the **window** in the room where they were playing fell out!! It just fell out and it wasn't windy at all." This was in **Rye Foreign.**

Rye Hospital has a strange story, related by Sister Winifred Wood in [RYE MEMORIES   VOLUME 23 : MEMORIES OF RYE AND WINCHELSEA AND DISTRICT MEMORIAL HOSPITAL.]

"I was on Night Duty and a lady from the Geographical Magazine was in the Private Ward. A patient in the Male Ward was dying. She said to me 'You've just had a man die? He's just passed through my room.' It was very eerie!"

Mrs Doris Carree used to work at Hill House Hospital and told us two ghost stories associated with it.

The old **Office Block**, now pulled down, had problems with the electrics. Appliances would be switched on and they would turn themselves off. This happened to everyone attempting to use the items, except **Mrs Joyce Beebe**. She could use any item for as long as she wished!!

The second incident was in the **Nurses Home**. A male nurse got up early one morning, before anyone else was about. He went to go into the toilet, but there was **a man** in there. He apologised and backed out to wait his turn. He waited for ages and then tried again, but no-one was there. The nurse would never go near there again!

Annabelle Alstin and **Jessie Franklyn** told us "A long time ago, during the War, children were evacuated to **Rye** and several went to live on **Rye Hill**. One of these was a girl called Mary. We were told her house was bombed and she had unfortunately died. Recently people have discovered children's toys, rocking horses, dolls, teddy bears etc. under Number 9 **Hill Top Drive**. Since then there have been stories of a young girl singing!"

[This house is one built on the site of The Rye Union Workhouse, which later became Hill House Hospital. Ed.]

STONE IN OXNEY

Georgina Drake wrote, "At my house in **Stone** there is a ghost. He is the former farmer and he lived until he was 23. He is normally quite nice and what happens is he repeatedly turns over the TV to nature programmes. He has swung on the chandelier twice."

UDIMORE

There is an ancient legend about the siting of Udimore Church. When St. Mary's Church was begun, it was being built on one side of a stretch of water or mere. Each night the building work disappeared and villagers waited up to see what had happened to the stones They described **hearing the rushing of angel's wings** as they carried the building materials 'Over the mere'. The Villagers decided to build it 'Over the mere' and it is where it is today. Udimore may mean 'Over the mere'.

Sam(antha) Jones told us "**The Kings Head Public House** dates back to 1535, when King Henry VIII was on the throne. I have lived there since 1988.

It all started one evening when my Dad (Trevor Jones) was locking up. He had just locked the front door when, all of a sudden, **a chair moved across the floor** on its own. I don't think Dad really believed what he saw, but when he thought about it, I think he started to realise that it wasn't his imagination. He also said that there was a mustard type **smell**."
Sam Jones 1995

Gemma Barker, Rebecca Edwards, Dale Goldsmith, Lettie Moon and Matthew Williams recorded this account. "A young girl went round to an old lady's house in **Udimore** and said 'Do you want any odd jobs doing?' The old lady said 'Yes, you can take my dog for a walk.' The girl was walking the dog along the main road and it got free and ran into the road. There were cars crashing and piling up and there was blood on the road. The girl thought the dog had been run over. She went back to the old lady's home and as she was crying, the lady said 'What are you crying about?' The girl replied 'Your dog has got run over.' But she looked past the lady and the dog sat there growling at her!"

WINCHELSEA

A friend was parking his car alongside **St. Thomas' Church** in Winchelsea, one quiet night, in the dark, when he heard the sound of **horses hooves** clattering on the road. He didn't open his car door, waiting for them to go past, but the sound got louder as it got to the car and then began to die away - but NO horses went by him!

Several people have told us about **hearing horses** coming up the **hill from the Strand Gate.**

One wrote to us "I was just going to go up through the **Strand Gate**, when I heard the **sound of several horses** coming up the hill fast. I quickly reversed the car and waited - and waited. No horses came under the Arch and the sounds just disappeared. I walked through to see if anything had happened to them, but there was nothing there. It was very eerie indeed."

The Weston Brothers, John and George, were two men in the eighteenth century, who by day were good citizens and wine merchants, but who, by night, were smugglers, horse-stealers and highwaymen. They would come up by this route into Winchelsea - perhaps it was them?

A headless man has been seen under **the trees in front of the Church.**

The next two stories come from a booklet written by **K.Forbes-Dunlop** 1988, called **Winchelsea Memories.**

"I heard of two strange happenings. One Christmas Eve, Mr Cook, (who lived at Cleveland House), had been out visiting friends and was on his way home taking **the path across the Churchyard** from the New Inn to Friars Road. It was midnight and very dark. As he drew near to the **Church porch**, he suddenly saw a pale, hazy light there. He stopped and watched. Out from the Church glided a **Grey Friar** carrying a dimly-lit lantern. The figure turned left to go down towards Friars Road, Mr Cook followed, keeping noiselessly on the grass. Out through the gate went the monk and Mr Cook followed. At his own home he paused and watched. The ghostly figure passed on to the Grey Friars.

The other story also concerns a strange light in the old **Church.** Late one night, a light was seen glimmering inside after it should have been closed. The observer hastened to find the sexton, who came hot foot to investigate. He found the entrance door unlocked and heard a tragic voice declaiming inside. On opening the door, he saw lights on the altar and the figure of a woman with upstretched arms, in the middle of the aisle, crying out. As he paused, he saw her fall flat. He ran hastily in to raise the prostrate form, only to discover it was the great **Ellen Terry**, rehearsing the part of **Lady Macbeth.**"

Another friend of the Editor told us of incidents in the house opposite to hers in **Friars Road**. A couple were living there and the wife saw **a man** in a suit and round tweed cap in the kitchen. Her husband laughed, until he, too, saw him. This occurred several times. The house in Winchelsea in which the Editor's friend was brought up, in **Castle Street**, had a **'presence'**. Her mother always said it was a pleasant 'feeling', but she did not like it. A Roman Catholic acquaintance also said, without prompting, that the house had an odd, uncomfortable feel about it. Some years later the lady had to spend five weeks on her back with an injury and the Vicar came in weekly to give her the Sacrament. The whole atmosphere became benign to her and the Roman Catholic friend, coming to visit her, immediately noticed the different 'feel' of the house.

Mr John Priestley said he can sense a **'presence'** on the landing of his home in **Winchelsea** sometimes. "It is a nice feeling," he says. "Although the house is a modern one, it is on the site of a very old one - perhaps 'it' has been inherited?"

WITTERSHAM

Andrew Grant Standen said "My Mum was left with some ghost books. One day there was a knocking in the porch. It sounded like someone chopping wood and then, in the night, she woke up with someone pushing her down into the mattress - she was pinned down and couldn't move. She thought it was something to do with the books, so she put them in a bin liner. The bin liner started to rustle as if there was something trying to get out of it. She gave the whole bag back to her brother, who owned the books."

OTHER STORIES FROM THE STUDENTS

Charlene Vidler told the story. "One day, Maryanne, Lisa and Shannon were baby-sitting for Mr Thomas's daughter, Ninna. Because Mr Thomas was going away to work, they had to baby-sit all night and all day. As he left he said 'Be good, Ninna!' They sat down and watched TV when they heard **a bang** upstairs. They looked at each other and they were scared. Shannon went upstairs but didn't see anything. They watched a bit more TV and the bang was heard again."

Danny Wilson said "When I was three, my Mum was doing the ironing. When she had finished, she turned the iron off. Later that night, she returned to the iron, to find it was on. The next night the same thing happened, but with the cooker. Ever since strange things like this have happened, but we have never got to the bottom of them."

One student wrote "In the Victorian era, our house was one of the main farming houses round our village. It is haunted by a man who wears all the farming clothes of that time and he smells of horses."

We close with a Cornish quotation:-
"From ghoulies and ghosties and long-leggety beasties
And things that go bump in the night,!
Good Lord, Deliver us !"

LOCAL HISTORY GROUPS

1986-1987
Michelle Robus
Kay Beeching
Stephen Tollett
Dean Blanshard
Tracy Champion
Denise Cotterell
John Green
James Kemp
Marie Pawson
Sharon Vidler

1987-1988
Michelle Robus
Kay Beeching
Stephen Tollett
Keith Williams
Samantha Jones
Zena Piggott
Louise Gilchrist
Mark Newnham
James Rosewell
Joseph Taylor
Elizabeth Cox
Joanna Pettifer
Emma Ashbee

1988-1989
Mark Newnham
Nigel Hammond
Gregory Coleman
Loraine Charman
Robert Ramsay
Barnaby Willard
Lisa Carder
Martin Phillips
Lisa Wilson
Lorraine Jury

1989-1990
Nigel Hammond
Gregory Coleman
Jonathon Breeds
James Eldridge
Christopher Apps
Tina Kennard
David Watts
Loraine Charman
Robert Ramsay
Sophie Crofts
Jane Cuthbert
David Standen
Andrew Gainsbury
Christopher Parsons

1990-1991
Loraine Charman
Robert Ramsay
Gregory Coleman
Jonathon Breeds
Andrew Gainsbury

1991-1992
Andrew Gainsbury
Penny Bell
Sarah Booth
Helen Robus
Donna Ripley
Matthew Collison
Steven Carter
Talya Bagwell
Helena Swaine
Phillip Pearce

1992-1993
Sarah Booth
Daryl Balcombe
Steven Field
Rae Newnham
Mark Smyth
Chris Wheeler
Jo Weekes

1993-1994
Vicky Beach
Jason Beckingham
Shelley Case
Julie Ennis
David Giles
Lisa Graham
Marie Hodgson
Jackie Lewis
Ian Potter
Hayley Rozier
Michelle Webb

Heidi Booth
Gina Bridgland
Lee Champion
Kevin Fuller
Lisa Goodsell
Claire Highams
Catherine Jung
Rebecca Mastin
Robin Pschenychka
Chris O'Shaugnessy
Loraine Charman

1994-1995
Vicky Beach
Kevin Fuller
Jackie Lewis
Georgina Pinwill
Lindsay Shipp
Andrew Tomkins

1995-1996
Hannah Brown
Claire Higham
Rosie Head
Samuel Jones
Alison Rowland

Paul Byrne
Laura Farley
Samantha Jones
Jackie Lewis
Steven Beach

Mrs Jo Kirkham, teacher of Geography and History, and Mayor of Rye 1979-1982, is the Co-Ordinator and Editor of the 'Rye Memories Series'